WASTING MONEY IS NOT FUNNY™

An Introductory Programmed Guide
to Understanding Personal Finance

New and Revised 3rd edition

Edward Deutscher, MD, MBA

Something About Communications

 ISBN 978-0-692-02526-0

Cover design and page layout by
Francisco Valcarcel: **franvalcarcel.com**

Cover illustration (hand with lighter) by
Nikita Konashenkov/Shutterstock.com.

Third edition published in 2019 by Something About Communications LLC. For enquiries, please contact:
faq@somethingaboutmedia.com

This book is a labor of love,
dedicated to all the people I met throughout
my medical career who told me that
"doctors don't know anything
about business or finance,"
which motivated me to pursue
the powerful knowledge offered by my
MBA program's faculty and staff.

Praise for Wasting Money Is Not Funny

A go-to guide for learning or refreshing yourself in the needed basics of finance that will help you in personal life, and in business

Mark C. Johnson, Esq.
(Attorney and Mechanical Engineer)

If you want to get a handle on your personal finances, read this book, then apply what you learn. This book painlessly puts you on the road to accumulating wealth!

Abdul-Sumi Dalal, Esq., B.B.A. in Finance

Wasting Money is Not Funny provides a great foundation to understand consumer finance in its most practical form. The only way not to be taken advantage of by an institutional lender in a monetary transaction is to be a knowledgeable borrower. The "PROGRAMMED LEARNING"exercises in Dr. Deutscher's course provide an efficient method to learning and retaining the necessary tools to be a formidable counterpart in any financial transaction. Learn the vitally important concepts of generating wealth by leveraging the time value of money and compound interest to truly understand how the rich get richer and how you can make these techniques work for you. Lastly, when faced with time sensitive financial decisions Wasting Money is Not Funny is written to automatically bring you back to a quick set of facts to arm you with the knowledge and demeanor necessary to win in every financial deal you engage in! I recommend this work for anyone who cares about not wasting money!

Bill Cibulas, J.D., Certified Financial Planner ™

If you want to get on top of your personal finance, read this book and do what it says. This book can make you seriously wealthy."

J. R Davis B.Sc

Please read this:

Programmed learning was popular many years ago, when I was in medical school. It is a very effective method to master new concepts, very quickly. In order to maximize the benefits of programmed learning, you must not jump around. Instead, please follow all the material in its presented order, from the beginning, to the end of the course.

Please do not look at any answers in advance. Review the introductory statement at the top of the page. The statement contains new vocabulary, material, and concepts. Carefully address each related question in sequence, one at a time, by filling in your answer(s), to a question. Base your answers on the introductory statements and previously covered material. You can check your answers for each question, by referring to the answers section, at the end of the book.

Once you understand the answer to a question, move on to the next question. If you have problems understanding the concepts addressed in a question, review the introductory statement at the top, along with relevant previously covered material. Do not proceed to the next question or statement, until you understand the concepts in every prior question, since you are building a foundation of knowledge.

If you think you can answer all the questions without the course, then congratulations! You will undoubtedly become a millionaire! However, if you are like most of us, you will be financially rewarded for the rest of your life by understanding the personal financial concepts presented in this introductory course.

Good luck!

Edward Deutscher, MD, MBA

WHAT WILL YOU GET BY THE END OF THIS BOOK?

If you use this programmed course as suggested, you will understand:

- terminology used every day in our personal financial lives
- interest, fees, loans, and other financial realities of our everyday personal finances
- how compound interest can be your best friend, or worst financial nightmare!
- how tools such as credit cards, checks, and ATM cards function
- advantages and risks associated with the use of common financial tools
- a basic financial philosophy to help achieve the goal of accumulating wealth, along with avoiding financial traps that ensnare many people, of all ages

Finance refers to the management of money and other assets. Personal finance refers to how individuals and families manage their money and other assets. Economy refers to everything related to the production and consumption of goods and services in an area, like a state or a country.

1. Any activity related to money is called ______________.

2. Finance involves earning, spending, or using ______________, in any way.

3. ______________ refers to the production and consumption of goods and services in a geographic area. It may involve money and other assets.

Understanding personal finance helps people avoid making costly mistakes, with their money! Learning personal finance helps people save more money.

4. People who don't learn about finance usually save less ______________.

5. People who don't want to waste their money learn about __________ finance.

6. Understanding personal finance teaches me how to manage my money and ensures that I will have more future ________

The only ways to legally acquire money are to earn it through work or investments, inherit it, or win the lottery.

7. Most people work to ________ their money.

8. If I have a landscaping service or become an executive, I will still have to ________ to earn money.

9. Very few people ________ enough to avoid work.

10. When I earn money, understanding personal ________ will help me be financially independent.

Income is receiving something of value, most often money that is earned over a specified period of time, such as an hour, day, week, month, year, or longer. Income can come from work, business, investments, and other sources

11. After college, I hope to find a good job to earn a high yearly ______.

12. People with higher education tend to have lifetime higher ______.

13. Personal incomes in some areas of the world are calculated using items such as livestock or crops, instead of ______. Income can be in any form that has value.

14. When my aunt was working, she saved money every month and now she lives comfortably on the income from her ______.

In our society, an expense is the cost or amount of money that needs to be paid for something of value. Common expenses include food, rent, books, tuition, insurance or other items purchased with money.

15. Tuition can be a major ________ for students and their parents.

16. Students often supplement scholarships and loans with ________ from part-time jobs.

17. Companies can have incomes and ________ in the millions (or billions) of dollars, every year.

18. Expenses can be small amounts of money for students, or billions of dollars per year for governments, but monies paid out are still ________.

A budget is an estimate of income and expenditures (monies paid for expenses) over a given or chosen period of time. Budgets must combine realistic estimates of income and expenses to be of value.

19. A realistic ________ is a helpful tool for students, whose only revenue (sources of money) is from scholarships, loans, family, and part-time jobs.

20. Businesses must create ________, in order to align their incomes and expenses. Businesses are in danger of failure, if expenses exceed revenues (total or gross income).

21. A person whose budget shows that ________ are higher than income needs to economize, by reducing spending to avoid debt.

22. The most difficult part of a personal budget is having the self-control to limit ________.

A wage is payment for a certain type of job or service that is usually paid by the hour (hourly).

23. If I earn $10 per hour mowing grass, the money I earn is called a ________.

24. The higher the wage, the more ________ I will earn per hour.

25. If the wage for cutting grass is $10 per hour, I will earn ________ in two hours.

26. If the wage for babysitting is $12 per hour, I will earn ________ in 30 minutes.

The fixed or agreed upon amount of money earned at regular intervals for doing a job (like weekly, monthly, or yearly) is called a salary. A salary is not earned by the hour.

27. If I agree to work at a job that pays a set (same) amount of money every week, my earnings are called a ________.

28. Wages are earned for a certain type of work, for an agreed unit of time (example: hour), but a ________ is usually paid every week, every other week (biweekly), twice a week (semiweekly), monthly, or yearly.

29. Semiweekly means twice a week, biweekly means every ______ weeks.

30. Elizabeth pays her employees a ________ of $12 per hour to cut grass.

31. Allison employs a gardener for a ________ of $250 a week to maintain the hedges and mow the grass, for the entire community.

An asset is something of economic value owned by a person, business, or government.

32. An asset is something of economic ________ that belongs to a person, business, or government.

33. Pamela's business owns three trucks that are the major ________ of her moving business.

34. The only ________ I have are my computer and college fund.

35. Mary's bakery owns the building and all the equipment needed to produce breads and cakes. These are the ________ of her business.

36. Assets are things that are owned that have ________ value.

A financial transaction is an agreement between a buyer and a seller to exchange or transfer assets that may include goods, services, or money. Value is what something is worth in money, materials, or services.

37. When Nuri sold Ian his iPad for $200, it was a personal financial ________ .

38. It was a major business ________ when Lily's business purchased the new building.

39. It was even a transaction when Sarah's lemonade stand ________ a cup of lemonade for 99 cents.

40. When Linda paid me $45 for mowing the grass, or a ________ of $15 per hour for three hours, the transaction was completed.

41. My labor cutting the grass has ________ that I can exchange for money. My labor is an asset.

An account is a record of financial transactions. Inventory is a record of all items currently in a business, store, or warehouse. Before computers, accounts and inventories were always handwritten. Accounts and inventories are now mostly electronic.

42. I keep an ________ of everything I earn babysitting, by writing every penny I earn in a notebook.

43. ________ is a record of all items currently in a store, business, or warehouse.

44. Inventories change through ________, such as sale(s) or shipment(s) of items.

45. When a store sells an item, it is a ________.

TRUE OR FALSE

46. It is also a transaction when a store purchases inventory for its shelves.

Rent is payment for use of an item or space for a specified period of time. An agreement to pay rent for the use of space is called a lease. The owner of the property is the landlord. The tenant (renter) may use the leased or rented space for business (commercial) or live in the property (residential), depending on the terms of the lease, also called a rental agreement.

47. A store maintains an ______ of everything it buys or sells in a computer file, in order to track its inventory.

48. ______ is usually paid monthly, for the use of a specific space.

49. Jose and his college roommates pay $1200 per month as ______ to live in a house.

50. Jon's ice cream shop pays $5000 monthly rent to use the store as specified in the ______ or rental agreement.

51. Rent is a recurring (repeating) payment for the use of a space, for an agreed upon duration of time that is outlined in the lease or ______ agreement.

The landlord receives monthly payments for the use of the leased space (asset). With a loan, the lender receives payments for the use of borrowed money (asset). Interest is the cost of borrowing (using) someone else's money. Renting can be thought of as paying (similar concept to interest) to use (borrow) someone else's space (asset).

52. The amount the lender charges to loan money to a borrower is called ________.

53. Jerome borrowed money from the bank to buy a car. The bank charged ________ (like rent, interest is payment for use of borrowed money, a different type of asset).

54. The bank and Jerome had a written agreement they both signed specifying the amount of ________ he had to pay the bank to use its money.

55. The person who borrows money pays interest, the person who lends money ________ (earns or charges) interest.

Money placed in a bank account earns interest that is paid by the bank to the account owner, a customer of the bank. Bank account, or just account, refers to a record of all transactions between the customer and the bank.

56. The record of all transactions between a customer and the bank is called an ________.

57. When you place money in a bank account, you are really lending the bank your money, so the bank pays you ________ to use your money. It's as if the bank rents or leases your money (your asset).

58. The bank is really ________ money from bank accounts at low interest rates, so it can ________ money to other customers at higher interest rates, in order to earn money for itself.

59. Rent is the cost for the ________ of space, like an apartment or store. ________ is the cost (like rent) for the use of someone else's money.

60. Money and property are both financial ________.

61. Interest and rent are similar to each other, because they are both payments for the use of someone else's ________.

When people have assets, the assets can earn money for the owner(s) without the owner(s) doing active work. The assets work to earn for their owners!

62. Marta's largest ________ is the $250 she deposited in her bank account.

63. I earn money on my bank account without working, because the bank pays me ________ to use my money (asset).

64. A tenant rents a condominium owned by Jazmin. Jazmin earns money without doing active work, because the tenant pays her for use of her ________.

65. ________ and ________ are two ways assets earn money, without the owners having to do active work.

The word 'principal' has several meanings. With loans, it is used to specify the original dollar amount of a loan, or the dollar amount remaining (outstanding or owed) on a loan that has not been totally repaid.

66. Benjamin borrowed $7500 from the bank to buy a car. He has repaid $1500. Six-thousand dollars is the outstanding (still owed) ________ (balance) on the loan that has not been repaid.

67. Thuy borrowed $50 from her parents to go on a school trip. If she repays $5 per week, after two weeks the outstanding principal (balance) on the loan will be ________.

68. Fran wants to buy my laptop. We agree the laptop is worth $350. If Fran gives me a $50 down payment and I agree to carry the remaining balance as a loan, ________ is the initial principal (balance) of the loan.

The amount of interest earned in a bank account is calculated using the interest rate (percent) the balance (dollars) in the bank account, and the period of time the money remains in the account. Interest accumulates over the duration of time the money remains in the bank account. In general, interest (dollars) can be calculated daily, monthly, or yearly. Interest ceases to be paid when all money has been withdrawn, from the bank account. Interest continues to be paid on the remaining money (balance) in the account, even after some of the money has been withdrawn, by the account owner.

We will now use some simplified examples to help understand interest concepts, by using what's referred to as "simple interest." In the real world, calculating interest on savings accounts is a bit more complicated, than as presented here. In reality, bank account interest calculations use yearly interest rates (percent) that are converted to daily interest rates (percent). This allows adjustments in calculations to accommodate deposits and withdrawals that can occur at any time. In the real world, interest on bank accounts is calculated as "compound interest."

Please focus on grasping the concepts of the presented simple interest (dollars) calculations. These examples assume no deposits into, or withdrawals from, the accounts. Interest will be calculated once, yearly. Remember, in the real world calculating bank account compound interest is much more complicated than the simplified examples presented here!

SIMPLIFIED SAVINGS ACCOUNT EXAMPLES:

69. To calculate the ________ earned for the first year on a bank account balance, multiply the yearly interest rate times the principal amount in the bank account.

70. If I deposit $100 in the bank, at an annual interest rate of 5% (0.05), I will earn $5 for the first year in ________________.

71. When I place money in a bank account,
I am ________________ the bank money.
They pay me ________________ to use (borrow) my money.

We can calculate the amount of interest paid/owed for a year by using the formula:
Interest = principal amount X annual interest rate X time (number of years).

I = Prt

The letters represent:

I = interest
P = principal amount (dollars)
r = annual interest rate (percent)
t = time (number of years)

SIMPLIFIED SAVINGS ACCOUNT EXAMPLES:

72. If Padmesh puts $200 dollars in the bank, at an annual interest rate of 5% (0.05), the bank will pay him ________ in interest, at the close of the first year.

73. Without having to actively work, Padmesh will have $210 at the end of the first year, because the bank paid him $10 in interest, on the $200 ________ in his account.

I deposited $100 in the bank, at an annual (yearly) interest rate of 5% (0.05).

SIMPLIFIED SAVINGS ACCOUNT EXAMPLES:

74. At the end of the first year, the bank will pay me ________ in interest.

75. At the end of the first year, the balance (principal) in my bank account will have grown to ________.

SIMPLE INTEREST CALCULATIONS:

I = Prt
I = $100 X 5% X 1 year = 100 X 0.05 X 1 = $5

The new principal amount after 1 year = (initial principal X interest rate X time) + (initial principal).

The new principal amount after 1 year = ($100 X 0.05 X 1) + $100 = $105.

Earning interest on an asset (something that has financial value) is really a gift. The asset itself does the work to earn you money!

SIMPLIFIED SAVINGS ACCOUNT EXAMPLES:

76. My friend and I each earned $1500 doing yard work, over summer vacation. I invested my money in a bank account. He wasted all his money on trivial things. The bank has an annual interest rate of 5% (0.05). At the end of the first year, the balance in my bank account was ________.

77. My friend had a balance of ________ at the end of the first year.

78. At the end of the first year, I removed the $75 interest from my bank account, after which I still had the original ________ amount of ________. I purchased video games and still had my summer work money. My friend had no money. My money worked for me to earn valuable interest.

WARNING: the next paragraphs contain the most difficult material in this introductory program. If it is too difficult to follow the first time over, please take away the concept that compound interest grows like an upside-down pyramid!

To compound means to combine. *Compound interest* continuously combines (adds) interest that is presently being earned, with the current principal (balance). The sum of the newly calculated interest and the existing principal (balance) will become the new principal (balance), to be used for the next interest calculation.

Current principal always includes the cumulative (ongoing) sum of the original principal (balance), *plus* all the interest that has already been earned. This process of calculating and adding newly earned interest to the ever-growing principal (balance), repeats itself at each of the agreed upon time intervals (daily, monthly, yearly).

When asked, Albert Einstein said the greatest invention in human history is *"compound interest!"*

SIMPLIFIED SAVINGS ACCOUNT EXAMPLES:

79. In an earlier example, the initial principal (deposit) of $100 in my bank account had grown to $105 after the first year. Therefore, the second year started with a new balance (principal) of ____ .

80. Using the interest formula, at the end of the second year the bank owes me ____ more in interest, at 5%.

EXPLANATION OF SIMPLIFIED SAVINGS ACCOUNT EXAMPLES:

Second year interest owed by bank = New principal X interest rate x 1 year
Second year interest owed by bank = $105 X 5% X 1 = 105 X 0.05 X 1 = $5.25

81. At the end of the second year, without working, I have a new balance in my bank account of ____, or $105 principal amount at the end of the first year, plus, the $5.25 interest earned at the end of the second year.

This is the magic of compounding! Interest is repeatedly calculated on principal that continues to grow, as the new interest is added to the principal. This new principal value is then used in the following interest calculations. It's basically interest on interest on interest on interest...

Compound interest demonstrates that time is valuable, in creating wealth!

Compounding of interest can make people wealthy, because their money works and grows for them.

EXAMPLE: You worked the summer of your junior year in high school and put your money in a bank account. The initial principal (deposited amount) was $1500. You decided to let the money remain in the bank account and compound. Six years later, when you graduate from college, you need the money from the bank account for a new car.

Through the magic of compounding, your balance has grown to $2010.14. You earned $510.14 in interest, without lifting a finger! That's over 33% growth of your money, just because of time.

$$I = Prt$$

End of Year	Principal ($)	Interest Rate	Interest Per Year ($)	Total Interest ($)
0	1500.00	0.05	0.00	0.00
1	1575.00	0.05	75.00	75.00
2	1653.75	0.05	78.55	153.75
3	1736.44	0.05	82.89	236.44
4	1823.26	0.05	86.82	323.26
5	1914.42	0.05	91.16	414.42
6	2010.14	0.05	95.72	510.14

SPOILER: if you can't calculate the numbers in the table, don't worry. This table was calculated using real life compounding, which is more complicated than our previous examples. Remember, compounding will make your money grow. Compounding is responsible for the magic of the "time value of money."

82. The last example demonstrates the ________ value of money.

83. Money grows over time, because the ________ compounds.

84. One of the best ways to create wealth is to take advantage of ___________, because it is responsible for the "*time value of money.*"

If you do not take advantage of compounding, you waste an opportunity to accumulate wealth!

So, let's look at this real-life example. A mixed or blended beverage at a coffeehouse costs around $4.75. The average is 180 schooldays per school year. If you purchase a mixed or blended beverage every day after school, you will spend $855 per year (six months).

Now let's see what happens if you invest the same amount of money, at a yearly compounding interest rate of 5%, instead of drinking the beverage five times a week, for six months of the year. If we start calculating from your second year of high school, at age sixteen, the following occurs:

After 11 years, at age 27, the money grows to $14,216

After 21 years, at age 37, the money grows to $34,450

That is beyond awesome! The cost of one mixed or blended beverage a day, five days a week, for only six months a year, compounds to these staggering amounts of money, because of the "time value of money!"

Your money works for you, if you invest it. Don't waste the financial gift of time!

Time is one of the most valuable assets for creating wealth!!! *

85. An ______ is something of financial value that is owned by a person, business, or government.

86. With ______ interest, money that is invested grows exponentially (faster and faster), over time.

87. ______ is what allows compounding to occur.

88. The time value of money is how invested money can create wealth through ______.

89. True or false: time is an important asset, in financial terms?

*Creating wealth is the formal way of saying 'getting rich'.

The time value of money can be more important than a large salary, for creating wealth.

90. In an earlier example, a principal amount left in the bank for six years, grew by over ____________, at 5% compound interest.

91. The over 33% growth occurred because of the __________ value of money.

92. Without the time value of money, a person would have to actively work to earn the over 33% growth that occurred passively (without working), in the earlier example due to __________ interest.

The time value of money can be more important than a large salary, for creating wealth!!

93. Who will get richer; a person who invests the same small amount of money every month, starting when he or she is 18, towards retirement, or a person with a big salary, who invests variable large amounts of money, starting when he or she is 35 or 40? (excludes lotteries, inheritance, and just dumb luck in business).

HINT: think coffeehouse beverage.

Advanced concept: the 18 year old is using an investment strategy referred to as dollar-cost averaging. He or she is an investment genius!

REVIEW: interest on your invested money is calculated by the formula: I = Prt.

The flip side is that the same formula is also used to calculate interest owed on loans.

The author apologizes from his heart, for the next two boring pages. However, please try to understand the concepts, since homes and cars are usually the two most expensive purchases people make during their lives.

Fixed rate loans have a fixed (always the same) interest rate that is used to calculate the total amount of interest owed, for the term (duration) of the loan. Car loans are usually fixed rate loans. There are other types of loans, where the interest rates may vary. Variable interest rate loans may be used in some types of mortgages. A mortgage is a type of loan used in real estate transactions, such as buying a home.

Amortization refers to debt (loan) repayment that follows a schedule of regular payments (installments) over a specified period of time (term). You will hear amortization used in reference to the schedule of repayments for mortgages and car loans. The repayment schedule is usually monthly, until the entire principal and interest of the loan are repaid.

In fixed rate car loans and fixed rate mortgages, although the total dollar amount of each monthly payment is the same, each monthly payment contains a part that goes towards interest payment, and a part that goes towards principal repayment. If you randomly examine any monthly payment for its principal and interest (P&I's) dollar amounts, the dollar amounts of the P&I's are not equal to the P&I's dollar amounts of any other monthly payment, despite the total monthly payment dollar amounts being equal, throughout the loan term.

In fixed rate car loans and fixed rate mortgages, monthly payments earlier in the life of the loans are mostly interest, with a small amount that goes towards principal repayment. This is referred to as "front-loaded." Later in the term of the loan, the monthly payments are mostly repayment of principal, since most of the loan interest has already been paid. This guarantees that the lender earns interest, before repayment of borrowed principal.

In contrast to fixed rate loans, compounding or joining of accrued (already earned or generated) interest and principal together, in order to create a new outstanding loan balance, is what causes the outstanding principal of a loan to grow exponentially. The accrued interest is continuously added to the previous loan principal. The new, ever growing loan principal is then used to calculate future owed interest, so the accrued interest generates additional future interest on itself!

Compound interest loans are dangerous for people who skip principal repayments, which allows the outstanding loan principal to grow exponentially, like our upside-down pyramid!

Borrowing money can be the evil twin of investing!

94. A convenient tool for creating wealth is the ________ ________ of money.

95. Money grows when we invest it, because of ________ ________.

96. When we borrow money, we owe ________ that is calculated using the ______ amount, interest rate, and duration (term) of the loan.

REFRESHER: interest owed on a loan may be calculated over any agreed upon time period, such as daily, weekly, monthly, or yearly.

REFRESHER: some loans have compound interest, not simple interest.

97. Would you prefer to borrow money that compounds daily or yearly?

Every time credit cards are used, card holders are actually borrowing money from the financial institutions (lenders) that issue the credit cards. Credit card companies purposely use short time intervals to calculate interest, so that it will compound quickly, against card holders.

98. Using credit cards is really ______________ from financial institutions that issue the credit cards.

99. A bank is a type of ______________ institution.

100. When an item is charged on a credit card, the cardholder is taking a loan from the issuing bank. The amount charged is the initial balance or ___________ of the loan.

101. In contrast to banks that ________ reasonably low interest rates on money loaned to them by bank account customers, banks _______ high interest rates on credit card balances that compound, over short time intervals.

The shorter the time interval and the higher the interest rate, the faster the outstanding (owed) loan balance compounds (grows).

Credit card users make banks and other financial institutions rich, by using short compounding intervals, combined with high interest rates that are applied to the outstanding balances, on credit cardholders accounts.

ARE THE FOLLOWING STATEMENTS TRUE OR FALSE?

102. Credit cards have very low interest rates

103. Interest calculated on credit card balances compounds yearly.

104. Interest on credit card balances may compound daily, which is why outstanding (owed) balances grow quickly

105. Unpaid credit card balances (outstanding) increase rapidly, because of frequent compounding, at high interest rates.

Financial institutions (like banks) charge high interest rates on their credit card loans that compound very rapidly. They simultaneously pay lower interest rates to their depositors on their bank accounts that compound slowly. This is an example of a series of financial transactions that yield nice profits for banks, based on the difference between credit card profits and interest paid to customers' accounts.

Credit card debt (outstanding balance) may compound over an astonishingly short time period.

106. Credit cards may have __________ rates well above 25% that can compound daily. This should be very scary to someone who can't pay the entire balance immediately, when the statement (bill) arrives.

107. At high interest rates, the amount of money owed grows very rapidly, especially with daily or monthly __________.

108. Charging goods or services on credit cards is, in reality, __________ from financial institutions at __________ interest rates, with rapid compounding.

Using credit cards is really just borrowing, with poor terms for the borrower.

109. True or false?

If you pay the balances on credit cards as soon as the statements arrive, you owe no interest*.

*(usually, but depends on terms of the credit card!)

HERE IS AN EXAMPLE OF THE DANGER OF USING CREDIT CARDS:

Earlier, we saw how $1500 would compound over 6 years in a bank account, at an annual interest rate of 5%. By the end of the sixth year, the bank had paid $510.14 in total interest to the depositor (account holder).

Now let's see what happens to the $1500 if you borrow it to purchase a laptop on a credit card, at a 25% interest rate that compounds daily.

The bank or other financial institution that issues the credit card always demands a minimum monthly payment. In this case, the minimum monthly amount you would be required to pay on your account would be $60.

At payments of $60 per month, at a 25% interest rate that compounds daily, the total amount spent to pay off the $1500 credit card loan would be **$9872.00, over six years!**

This is not an exaggeration, but is an accurate calculation of the cost of borrowing money on credit cards.

Using credit cards is a terrible way to borrow money. In the earlier example, after 6 years the bank paid $510.14 in total interest on a deposit (starting principal balance) of $1500 that was placed in a savings account. The balance in the account grew to $2010.14.

In the last example, the credit card user (borrower) ultimately gave the bank $9872.00 in total payments, over the same time period, with the same starting principal balance of $1500.

Credit card use is basically borrowing, with very bad terms. The financial institutions stack the deck against their customers, to earn profits.

110. ________ may refer to the duration of a loan, such as a car loan, and terms may refer to what is specified in a loan agreement.

111. Using credit cards is really just borrowing with very bad ________, because of high interest rates and rapid compounding.

112. Credit cards can be dangerous to the financial future of the card user, because of high ________ rates and rapid ________.

There is a way to use credit cards safely, but it is usually not an option for young people, with limited incomes.

113. Many credit cards allow a grace period of one month or less, without interest charges, if the entire balance is __________ in full, before the end of the grace period.

114. If the entire credit card balance is paid immediately, when the monthly statement (bill) arrives, the bank is actually giving the card holder an __________ -free loan. Not all credit cards offer this privilege.

115. Credit cards are convenient for business travelers, who pay the entire balance immediately when monthly credit card ____________________ arrive.

With a credit card, the financial institution lends its money to the card user and charges exorbitant interest. With debit cards (e-cards), money is transferred electronically from the card user's own savings or checking account.

116. When a credit cardholder uses a credit card to pay for something, the bank ________ money to the cardholder.

117. Banks and other financial institutions charge ________ on the money they loan to their cardholders.

118. With debit cards, there is no ________ assessed to users, because there is instantaneous electronic transfer of money, from the cardholder's own ________.

119. E-card use is an electronic ________ of the cardholder's own money, and not a loan from the financial institution.

120. Like a checking account, there may be ________ and fees associated with the use of debit cards.

Loans may be 'secured' by an asset that the lender can seize, if the loan is not repaid. The asset is called collateral. Unsecured loans are not backed by collateral that can be seized for non-repayment. Secured loans have lower interest rates than unsecured loans, which is advantageous to the borrower(s). Secured loans have less risk for the lender.

121. With a ________ loan, the borrower designates an asset as collateral. The lender can seize the asset, if the loan is not repaid on time, so there is less financial risk for the lender.

122. A car loan is an example of a ________ loan because the bank can repossess (take) the car, if the loan payments are not made ________.

123. A credit card loan is an example of an ________ loan.

124. Without an asset to repossess, there is ________ to the lender, if the borrowed money is not repaid.

In the financial world, including personal finance, the higher the risk, the higher the possible return (earnings) on an investment. However, the higher the risk, the higher the chance of losing an investment. When institutions loan money, they are making in investment, where the interest is the return (earnings) on their investment. Unsecured loans have higher risk, and therefore higher returns on investment (ROI) for the lender. Unsecured loans cost the borrowers more, because they must pay a risk premium (higher cost) to the lender.

125. The bank charges higher interest rates on credit card loans, because they are __________ and the bank wants to be compensated for taking risk.

126. A risk premium is an additional cost, above the regular interest that is charged to borrow money. Unsecured loans usually require a __________ premium that is paid by the borrower.

127. People who have bad credit histories that come from defaulting (not paying) previous loans, evictions, or other previous financial problems, are considered bad risks by lenders. Lenders will only loan money at high interest rates, to people with bad credit histories. High interest rates are a type of __________ premium.

NOTE: there are times when people have bad credit ratings due to financial circumstances that were outside their control. Nevertheless, they are still considered high financial risks by lending institutions, so they can only borrow at higher interest rates.

Secured loans are more economical for the borrower, because the borrower offers collateral (an asset), to secure the loan

128. Unsecured loans have more ______ for the lender.

129. The more the risk for the lender, the higher the ______ rate, as it includes a risk premium.

130. ________ is the asset used to secure a loan.

131. In a car loan, the vehicle is used as ________.

132. A mortgage on a house is a type of ________ loan. The collateral for the loan is the ________.

133. Interest rates are ______ for collateralized loans.

A check is an instrument (financial term) that orders payment from a checking account that has been funded (deposited money into) by the check writer. If a check is written for more than the account balance, it is called an overdraft (from the verb 'overdraw').

134. If I write a check to my friend, the check orders my bank to ________ my friend the check amount, from my ________ ________.

135. There must be enough ________ in my checking account, to cover the amount of the check.

136. My bank will not ________ (go negative in) my checking account, by paying a check for more than my checking account balance (funds in the account).

137. Some banks will ________ accounts, by paying checks valued at more than account balances. Those banks charge overdrawn customers penalties, interest, and deduct ________ from the accounts, as soon as the customers deposit more funds into the accounts.

138. Checks have to be ________, often by hand.

139. The recipient of a check must deliver the check to a bank for ________.

140. When the check recipient deposits the check in his/her bank, his/her bank arranges a money transfer, from the check writer's ________.

141. When the recipient of a check deposits it in his/her bank, there is often a delay (or hold) on the funds, until the check________ (funds are available).

142. The time required for the funds to transfer between banks is why there is a delay for the check to ________, before the funds are available in the recipient's account.

Financial institutions charge for the use of their services. A fee is the price one pays for the bank's services.

143. When a credit card is used, the bank __________ interest.

144. In addition to interest, many banks and financial institutions charge __________ that customers must pay for the privilege of using their credit cards, or other banking services.

145. Many of the __________ are hidden or disguised on monthly bank statements, so customers are often unaware of the total amount they are paying in fees.

146. If a checking account is overdrawn, because checks are written for more than the account __________, the bank may charge the customer punishing overdraft __________.

Checking accounts often require minimum balances. Some banks charge heavy fees if an account balance falls below the minimum required balance, even by one cent!

Low balance fees may be triggered due to a drop in an account balance that was caused by other charges and fees that were assessed, by the bank itself! It's legal. The bank can deduct charges and fees from an account that causes the account balance to fall below the minimum requirement, and then assess (apply) steep overdraft fees and penalties to the account, because the account balance dropped below the minimal required balance.

147. Unlike savings accounts that pay __________ on the account balance, checking accounts usually don't pay interest and usually have associated ______.

148. Unlike __________ accounts, __________ accounts cannot be __________ by removing more money than the account balance.

149. If all the money is _______ from a savings account, the account is automatically _________, by the bank.

150. If a check is written for more than the _________ in a checking account, the account is said to be ____________ and fees, penalties, or both may be charged by the bank.

Individual savings accounts earn interest, because the account owner lends the bank the money that is deposited in the savings account. Checking accounts cost the account owner money, because the bank provides services to the checking account owner that have associated fees. A checking account is not an investment that earns money.

151. The ______ value of money helps money grow through the magic of ______.

152. The time value of money does not apply to ______ accounts.

153. A savings account is a type of ______, because it earns interest.

154. A checking account offers ______. It does not usually earn ______.

155. A checking account is used for the convenience of its services, but not as an ______.

A debit is a charge or quantity of money that is deducted from an account.

156. When I don't watch my checking account balance, I may ________ the account by writing checks for more money than I have in the account.

157. When a checking account is overdrawn, the bank charges ________. The bank will ________ my account to collect fees and overdraft charges (penalties).

158. When I withdraw money from my savings account, the account is ________, and the account balance drops by the amount of the ________.

A debit card (ATM, bank card, e-card) allows the cardholder electronic access to his or her account, at a financial institution, such as a bank. A bank card (ATM card) may be used at ATM's (automated teller machines). Many banks charge fees for the use of ATM's.

A payer (payor) pays for goods or services, a payee receives the payment.

159. A __________ card provides the cardholder with immediate __________ access to his or her account.

160. A ________ card can be swiped to pay for goods or services, such as at a store checkout.

161. The bank transfers money from the __________ account, to the account of the __________.

162. The shopper is the __________.

163. The store is the __________.

Credit cardholders are usually not responsible for most of the fraudulent charges placed on their lost credit cards, but only if the credit card loss is promptly reported to the financial institution that issued the card. Debit cardholders may be responsible for all charges placed on their lost debit cards. They can lose all the money in their accounts, through unauthorized use of their debit/bank/e-cards!

164. There may be associated ________ the cardholder must pay for the privilege of using a debit card.

165. Debit cards usually cannot be ________, because funds are ordinarily not electronically transferred if there is not enough money in the account to cover a payment request.

166. With a lost ________ card, the cardholder's account is responsible for all fraudulent charges made with the lost card, during the time period preceding the card being reported as lost, to the bank.

167. With a lost ________ card, the cardholder's account is not responsible for fraudulent charges (usually above $50), if the loss of the card is reported to the card's financial institution, as soon as possible.

A ledger is a written or computer file that records all financial transactions of an account.

168. A __________ is a record of the date, amount, and number of each check that is written by the owner of a checking account.

169. When a check is __________ by the check recipient, the check writer's bank deducts the amount of the check, from the check writer's account.

170. The owner of a checking account must record each check and debit card transaction in the account ledger, to avoid accidental __________ of the account, due to insufficient funds.

171. If accounts are overdrawn, there may be __________ and penalties charged to the accounts.

Reconciliation is the comparison of two sets of financial records, in order to ensure that they agree (reconcile). Banks issue monthly individual account statements that list all financial transactions that occurred during the month. Bank statements are issued for savings, checking, debit, and credit card accounts. Statements may be paper or electronic.

172. At the end of each month, financial institutions (like banks) send __________ to account owners that list all financial transactions that occurred in their accounts, during the month.

173. A statement is the bank's version of an account __________. A personal ledger should be accurately maintained by the account owner.

174. The bank statement also indicates __________ that the bank has deducted, as fees from the account balance.

175. The owner's ledger and the bank statement (ledger) must be compared by the account owner, to make sure they are in agreement. This is called balancing the checkbook or __________.

Account owners must reconcile their personal ledgers, with monthly bank statements. Banks deduct fees from accounts, which may cause the account balance to become overdrawn, triggering additional fees and penalties. Also, banks and credit card companies do make mistakes! Customers must be alert and protect themselves from potential costly overdrafts and bank errors.

176. A financial institution may impose heavy ______ for an overdrawn account, because there may be significant overdraft penalties.

177. The bank fees and penalties may be larger than the actual amount that the account was originally ______.

178. In addition to fees and penalties charged to overdrawn accounts, banks may charge ______ on the original overdrawn amounts, plus, interest on the ______ fees and penalties. This can be viewed as a financial double whammy! Banks consider unpaid charges and penalties as loans to the account owner.

179. Fees, overdraft penalties, and the ______ charged on them, cost the account owners lots of money and create ______ for financial institutions.

Investment is the use of financial assets to earn returns (money). Investments are the use of money, with the expectation, over time, of financial gain.

180. __________ is the intelligent use of money, with the expectation of earning returns (money) on investment (ROI).

181. A bank account that pays __________ is an example of an investment.

182. Purchase of a property that pays __________, is also an investment.

183. The purchase of an empty lot that is located in a desirable neighborhood may be a good investment, even though there is no __________ initially, because the value of the property should __________ over time.

The "time value of money" continues to sneak back, so, it must be very important in creating wealth!

Remember, with few exceptions the only legal ways to acquire wealth are to earn it, inherit it, or win the lottery.

184. Like most people, I am going to have to ________ money, to become wealthy.

185. I can ________ to earn money, but I can also invest money to create ________ for myself.

186. In financial terms, ________ has significant value.

187. Taking advantage of the time ________ of money is one of the best ways to become rich.

188. Remember, money grows through the magic of ________, over time!

Money that is carefully invested will grow, through the time value of money. Gambling is risking something of value (like money) on events with uncertain, uncontrollable outcomes.

189. Any money invested where it will earn interest, will grow because of the time ______ of money, through the ______ ______ ______.

190. Investments must be researched for security and growth potential, or else your money is just being ______.

191. Speculation is the term used for ______, with risky ______.

192. The time value of money works well, when there are scheduled interest payments that ______. Other types of investments, such as real estate, must be thoroughly researched and evaluated for security and future growth potential, which can be more difficult than evaluating compound interest payments.

WHAT ARE THE SECRETS TO BECOMING WEALTHY INSTEAD OF WASTING MONEY?

193. Start to invest (save) early, to take advantage of the ______ ________ __ ________.

194. The time value of money works, through the magic of ________.

195. If possible, avoid loans, especially unsecured high interest loans, such as _____ _____, because they compound quickly for the bank, against you!

196. Credit cards are just very expensive ways to ______ money.

SECRETS OF BECOMING WEALTHY INSTEAD OF WASTING MONEY, CONTINUED.

197. Credit card use can be dangerous, because of high interest rates and hidden ______ that compound against you quickly.

198. Be careful to secure ______ ______, because the cardholder is responsible for fraudulent charges.

199. Make a contract with yourself that when you earn money, you will always invest (save) a certain percentage or specific dollar amount, before you start to spend, in order to take advantage of the ______ ______ of money.

200. True or False:

If I follow the above suggestions, I have the opportunity to become wealthy (rich), at a young age.

HERE ARE FOUR SUGGESTIONS TO HELP PEOPLE AVOID WASTING MONEY, IN ORDER TO ACCUMULATE WEALTH.

1. Master the personal financial terms and concepts presented in this book. They will serve you, for your entire life!

2. Start putting away money, instead of spending, as early as you can, in order to take advantage of the ***time value of money!***

3. Always invest a fixed dollar amount, or fixed percentage of your earnings, before you spend on anything else. This is sometimes referred to as 'paying yourself first,' or technically as dollar-cost averaging. Make this a habit for life!

4. Avoid using costly loans, such as credit cards that have lots of charges and high interest rates that rapidly compound against you. Credit cards compound for the banks, at your expense! Credit cards are the kiss of death, for people who want to accumulate wealth!

ANSWERS

1. finance
2. money
3. Economy
4. money
5. personal
6. savings
7. earn
8. work
9. inherit
10. finance
11. income
12. incomes
13. money
14. savings
15. expense
16. income
17. expenses
18. expenses
19. budget
20. budgets

21. expenses
22. spending
23. wage
24. money
25. $20
26. $6
27. salary
28. salary
29. two
30. wage
31. salary
32. value
33. assets
34. assets
35. assets
36. economic
37. transaction
38. transaction
39. sold
40. wage

41. value
42. account
43. Inventory
44. transactions
45. transaction
46. True
47. account
48. Rent
49. rent
50. lease
51. rental
52. interest
53. interest
54. interest
55. receives
56. account
57. interest
58. (a) borrowing, (b) loan
59. (a) use, (b) Interest
60. assets

61. asset(s)
62. asset
63. interest
64. asset
65. (a) interest, (b) rent
66. principal
67. $40
68. $300
69. interest
70. interest
71. (a) lending, (b) interest
72. $10
73. principal
74. $5
75. $105
76. $1575
77. $0.00
78. (a) principal, (b) $1500
79. $105
80. $5.25

81. $110.25
82. time
83. interest
84. compounding
85. asset
86. compound
87. Time
88. compounding
89. True
90. 33% (1/3)
91. time
92. compound
93. the 18-year-old
94. (a) time, (b) value
95. (a) compound, (b) interest
96. (a) interest, (b) principal
97. Yearly
98. borrowing
99. financial
100. principal

101. (a) pay, (b) charge
102. False
103. False
104. True
105. True
106. interest
107. compounding
108. (a) borrowing (b) high
109. True
110. Term
111. terms
112. (a) interest, (b) compounding
113. paid
114. interest
115. statements (or bills)
116. lends
117. interest
118. (a) interest, (b) account
119. transfer
120. charges

121. secured
122. (a) secured, (b) on time,
123. unsecured
124. risk
125. unsecured
126. risk
127. risk
128. risk
129. interest
130. Collateral
131. collateral
132. (a) secured, (b) house
133. lower
134. (a) pay, (b) checking, (c) account
135. funds (money)
136. overdraw
137. (a) overdraw, (b) fees
138. written
139. payment
140. bank

141. clears
142. clear
143. charges
144. fees
145. fees
146. (a) balance, (b) fees
147. (a) interest, (b) fees
148. (a) checking, (b) savings, (c) overdrawn
149. (a) withdrawn, (b) closed
150. (a) balance, (b) overdrawn
151. (a) time, (b) compounding
152. checking
153. investment
154. (a) services, (b) interest
155. investment
156. overdraw
157. (a) fees, (b) debit
158. (a) debited, (b) withdrawal
159. (a) debit (or bank), (b) electronic
160. debit

161. (a) payor's, (b) payee (recipient)
162. payor
163. payee
164. fees
165. overdrawn
166. debit
167. credit
168. ledger
169. cashed
170. overdrafts
171. fees
172. statements
173. ledger
174. charges
175. reconciliation
176. fees
177. overdrawn
178. (a) interest, (b) overdraft
179. (a) interest, (b) wealth
180. Investment

181. interest
182. rent
183. (a) rent, (b) increase (appreciate)
184. earn
185. (a) work, (b) wealth
186. time
187. value
188. compounding
189. (a) value, (b) magic of compounding
190. gambled,
191. (a) gambling, (b) investments,
192. compound
193. time value of money,
194. compounding
195. credit cards
196. borrow
197. fees
198. debit cards
199. time value
200. True

ACKNOWLEDGEMENTS

Without the unequivocal, ever present, non-judgmental support of my wife Nahid Arasteh, and her two sisters, Mahshid, and Mehregan, I would never have been able to complete this programmed learning text. Having written technical pieces, I was unprepared for the inherent difficulties and uniqueness related to writing a self-contained, programmed learning text that flows, while remaining non-intimidating. My wife and her family's encouragement and support were the ingredients that allowed me to sit, hour after hour, re-wording and refining sentence after sentence, concept after concept, on top of a schedule already dominated by the monumental demands of a mature ophthalmology practice, co-managing our real estate, and working on patents.

Two Professors at the University of Tennessee MBA program, Philip Daves, Ph.D (Finance) and Charles Noon, Ph.D (Operations and Management Sciences) taught me concepts that changed my thought processes in ways that that are evident throughout the entire text. Without their profound influences, it would have been inconceivable for me to even consider addressing peoples' difficulties with the daily basics of personal finance, as well as many other ongoing projects, in my personal business life.

Lastly, this project would never have been possible, without the efforts of my British friends and colleagues. Thank you to the team at Something About Media, including Sarah, Ian, and Lily, who along with Jon helped to coordinate and publish the text. Special thanks also goes to Francisco Valcarcel of Spain and Germany, for the lovely artwork and graphic designs.

Sincerely,
Edward Deutscher, MD, MBA

ABOUT THE AUTHOR

Dr. Edward Deutscher was educated in the United States and Europe. He holds medical degrees from the Vrije Universiteit te Brussel and Albert Einstein College of Medicine, in New York City. He received his MBA from the University of Tennessee.

Dr. Deutscher practiced eye surgery, for many years. He lives in Florida with his wife, Nahid, who is a practicing engineer, as well as his business and real estate partner.

Dr. Deutscher has extensive business experience that includes business administration, healthcare policy, small business management, medical practice management, real estate investment, and finance.

In addition to his medical career, Dr. Deutscher holds several medical and non-medical patents. He was host of a successful radio talk show, and authored a chapter in an ophthalmic surgical textbook.

Made in the USA
Monee, IL
04 November 2026

67382351R00046